PIANO • VOCAL • GUITAR

WORSHIP TOGETHER

SONGS YOU KN

25 FAVORITE WORSHIP SONGS

ISBN 978-1-4584-0012-3

HAL•LEONARD® CORPORATION
7777 W. Bluemound Rd. P.O. Box 13819 Milwaukee, WI 53213

AMAZING GRACE
(My Chains Are Gone)

Words by JOHN NEWTON
Traditional American Melody
Additional Words and Music by CHRIS TOMLIN
and LOUIE GIGLIO

G
C(add2)/G
G
grace that taught my heart to fear, and grace my fears re-
Lord has prom-ised good to me, His Word my hope se-
D/G
G
G(add2)/B
C(add2)
G
lieved. How pre-cious did that grace ap-pear the
cures. He will my shield and por-tion be as
D/G
G
C/G
G
C
hour I first be-lieved. My chains are gone, I've been set
long as life en-dures.
mf
G/B
C
free. My God, my Sav-ior has ran-somed

G/D
G/B
C
me. And like a flood, His mer - cy
G/B
D7sus/A
D7sus
1 G
rains un - end - ing love, a - maz - ing grace.
mp
D/G
G
D/G
The
2 G
G/B
C
G/B
grace. My chains are gone, I've been set free. My God, my
mf

C/E
G/D
Sav - ior has ran - somed me. And like a
C
G/B
flood, His mer - cy rains un - end - ing
D7sus/A
D7sus
G
C/G
G
love, a - maz - ing grace. The
mp
Gsus
3fr
G
earth shall soon dis - solve like snow, the sun for - bear to

D/G G Gsus2/B Csus2 G
3fr
shine. But_ God, who_ called__ me here be - low will
D/G G C/G G D/G
be for - ev - er mine, will be for - ev - er
G C/G G D/G G
mine. You are for - ev - er mine.
rit.

BEAUTIFUL ONE

Words and Music by
TIM HUGHES

B♭
Csus
3fr
Dm7
cross has spo - ken mer - cy o - ver me.
might - y works dis - played for all to see.
B♭
Csus
3fr
No eye has seen, no ear has heard, no
The beau - ty of Your maj - es - ty a -
F/A
B♭
heart can ful - ly know how glo - ri - ous, how
wakes my heart to sing: How mar - vel - ous, how
C
F
beau - ti - ful You are.
won - der - ful You are.
3
Beau - ti - ful
3
cresc.

B♭
C
B♭
One I love, Beau - ti - ful One I a -
f
C
B♭
To Coda
C
dore, Beau - ti - ful One, my soul must
F
1
2
D.S. al Coda
sing. Beau - ti - ful
CODA
C
Gm7(add4)
soul must sing.

Csus
C
Csus2
C
Gm7(add4)
Csus
C
Csus2
C
Beau - ti - ful
Gm7
One.
Csus
C
Csus2
C
Beau - ti - ful
Gm7
One.

Csus
C
B♭sus2
You o - pened my eyes to Your won -
mp
Csus
B♭sus2
Csus
- ders a - new, You cap - tured my heart with this love, 'cause noth -
B♭sus2
Csus
F
- ing on earth is as beau - ti - ful as You.
And You o -
mf
B♭
C
B♭/D
- pened my eyes to Your won - ders a - new, You cap - tured my heart with this

C/E
Bb
C
love, 'cause noth - ing on earth is as beau - ti - ful as You.
F
N.C.
Bb
C
Beau - ti - ful One I love, Beau - ti - ful
f
Bb
C
Bb
C
One I a - dore, Beau - ti - ful One my soul must
F
1
2
sing. Beau - ti - ful Beau - ti - ful

Bb C Bb/D C/E
One I love, Beau - ti - ful One I a - dore, Beau - ti - ful
Bb C F
One my soul must sing.
Bb F/C Bb/D
C/E Bb C C7 F

BLESSED BE YOUR NAME

Words and Music by MATT REDMAN
and BETH REDMAN

* *Recorded a half step lower.*

G6
be Your name.
be Your name.
D
A
Bless - ed be Your name when I'm
Bless - ed be Your name on the
Bm7
G
found in the des - ert place, though I
road marked with suf - fer - ing, though there's
D
A
walk through the wil - der - ness, bless - ed
pain in the of - fer - ing, bless - ed

G(add2)
D
be Your name.
be Your name.
Ev - 'ry bless - ing
A
Bm7
G
You pour out I'll turn back to praise.
D
A
Bm7
When the dark - ness clos - es in, Lord, still I will
G
D
A
say: Bless - ed be the name of the Lord, bless - ed be Your

Bm7
G
D
name.
Bless - ed be the name of the Lord,
Asus
Bm7
1 G
blessed - ed be Your glo - ri - ous name.
2 G(add2)
D
A
You give and take a - way, You
Bm7
G
D
give and take a - way.
My heart will choose to

A
Bm7
G
say, "Lord, bless - ed be Your name."
D
A
Ev - 'ry bless - ing You pour out I'll
Bm7
G
D
turn back to praise. When the dark - ness
A
Bm7
G
clos - es in, Lord, still I'm gon - na say: Bless - ed be the

D
A
Bm7
name of the Lord, bless - ed be Your name, Je -
G
D
A
sus. Bless - ed be the name of the Lord, bless - ed be Your
Bm7
G
D
glo - ri - ous name. Bless - ed be the name of the Lord,
A
Bm7
G
bless - ed be Your name. Bless - ed be the

D
Asus
Bm7
name of the Lord, bless - ed be Your glo - ri - ous name.
G
D
A
You give and take a - way, You
Bm7
G
D
give and take a - way. My heart will choose to
A
Bm7
G
D(add2)
say, "Lord, bless - ed be Your name." Yeah, yeah.

BETTER IS ONE DAY

Words and Music by
MATT REDMAN

E5
Asus2
here my heart is sat - is - fied with - in Your pres -
thing I ask and I would seek: to see Your beau -
E5
- ence. I sing be - neath the shad - ow of Your
- ty, to find You in the place Your glo - ry
Bsus
Asus2
wings.
dwells.
Bet-ter is one day in Your courts, bet-ter is
Bsus
Asus2
A/C♯
one day in Your house, bet - ter is one day in Your courts than thou - sands

Bsus
E/G♯
Asus2
else - where. Bet - ter is one day in Your courts, bet - ter is
Bsus
Asus2
A/C♯
To Coda
one day in Your house, bet - ter is one day in Your courts than thou - sands
1
Bsus
E5
else - where, than thou - sands else - where.
2
Bsus
C♯m7
4fr
B
One else - where. My heart and flesh cry out

Asus2
Bsus
C♯m7
4fr
Asus2
Bsus
for You, the liv - ing God. Your Spir - it's wa - ter to my soul.
C♯m7
4fr
B
Asus2
E/G♯
I've tast - ed and I've seen. Come once a - gain to me. I will draw near to You,
F♯m7
Bsus
I will draw near to You, to You.
Asus2
Bsus
Asus2

C/E F C/E F G
up - on the Lord. Our God, You reign for - ev -
Am G C/E F C/E F
- er. Our Hope, our strong
G Am G Gsus
De - liv - er - er.
C F
You are the ev - er - last - ing God, the ev -

Am
- er - last - ing God. You do not faint, You
F
G/F
Fmaj7
C
won't grow wea - ry. You're the de - fend -
F
- er of the weak, You com - fort those in need,
Am
F
G/F
You lift us up on wings like

1
Fmaj7
ea - gles.
2
Fmaj7
ea - gles.
C
F
Am
F
1
2
C
You are the ev -
mp subito

F
- er - last - ing God, the ev - er - last - ing God,
Am
F
the ev - er - last - ing God, the ev -
cresc.
C
- er - last - ing. Strength will rise as we wait up - on the Lord, wait
f
F
Am
up - on the Lord, we will wait up - on the Lord. Strength will rise as we wait

F
upon the Lord, wait upon the Lord, wait upon the Lord.
C
F
You are the everlasting God, the ev-
Am
-erlasting God, the everlasting God,
F
C
the everlasting.

FOREVER

Words and Music by
CHRIS TOMLIN

A
bove all things. His love endures forever.
been reborn, His love endures forever.
carry on. His love endures forever.
Sing
E
praise,
Dsus2/F♯
sing praise.
1
2, 3
Sing
E
praise,
Dsus2/F♯
sing praise.
Yeah, forev -

A
F#m7
- er God is faith - ful. For - ev - er God is strong.
Esus
To Coda
For - ev - er God is with us, for - ev -
Dsus2
A
- er, for - ev - er.
D.S. al Coda
(take 2nd ending)

CODA
Dsus2
A
-er and ev-er and ev-er. For-ev-er God is faith-
F♯m7
-ful. For-ev-er God is strong. For-ev-
Esus
Dsus2
-er God is with us, for-ev-er, for-ev-
A
-er, for-ev-er.

FROM THE INSIDE OUT

Words and Music by
JOEL HOUSTON

C G Am Fmaj7
in Your grace. Ev - er - last - ing, Your light will shine when
- ing You praise.
C G Am Fmaj7
all else fades. Nev-er-end - ing, Your glo - ry goes be - yond all fame.
1
C G
F(add2) C G F(add2)
C G
Your will a -
2, 3
C G F(add2)
yond all fame. In my heart and my soul,

C
Am7
Gsus
3fr
well, I give You con - trol.
Con - sume me from the in - side out, Lord.
F(add2)
Am7
Gsus
3fr
To Coda
And let jus - tice and praise
be - come my em - brace,
to love You from the
Dm7
Dm9
3fr
F(add2)
in - side out.
C
G
F(add2)
C
G
D.S. al Coda
(take 2nd ending)
Your will a -

CODA
Dm7
Am
Fmaj7
C
G
in - side out. Ev-er-last - ing, Your light will shine when all else fades. Nev-er-end -
f
Am
Fmaj7
C
G
C
F
- ing, Your glo-ry goes be - yond all fame. And the cry of my heart is to bring
G
Am
F
G
F
G
You praise. From the in - side out, Lord, my soul cries out, Lord.
F
C

Am
C/G
Fmaj7
Am
G(add2)
Dm7
F(add2)
C
Am7
In my heart and my soul, well, I give You con - trol. Con - sume me from the
mp

Gsus
3fr
F(add2)
Am7
in - side out, Lord. Let jus - tice and praise ___ be - come my em - brace, _
cresc. poco a poco
Gsus
3fr
Dm7
Am
Fmaj7
___ to love You from the in - side out. Ev - er - last - ing, Your light will shine when
f
C
G
Am
Fmaj7
C
G
all else fades. Nev - er - end - ing, Your glo - ry goes be - yond all fame. And the cry _

C
F
G
Am
of my heart is to bring You praise. From the in -
F
G
1
F
G
2
F
G
- side out, Lord, my soul cries out. Ev - er - last - cries out, from the in -
F
G
F
G
Fsus2
- side out, Lord, my soul cries out, Lord.

GLORY TO GOD FOREVER

Words and Music by STEVE FEE
and VICKY BEECHING

* Recorded a half step lower.

C G C/E F
en - throned a - bove all things. An - gels and saints cry out;
a blaz - ing of - fer - ing, a life that shouts and sings
C G F C G Am7
we join them as we sing: Glo - ry to God, glo - ry to God,
the great - ness of our King.
F C G F C
glo - ry to God for - ev - er. Glo - ry to God,
G Am7 F C
glo - ry to God, glo - ry to God for - ev - er,
1
G
yeah.

2
G F C G Am
Take my life and let it be all for You and for Your glo - ry.
F C G F C
Take my life and let it be Yours. Take my life and let it be
G Am F C G
all for You and for Your glo - ry. Take my life and let it be Yours. We sing:
F C G Am7 F C
Glo - ry to God, glo - ry to God, glo - ry to God for - ev - er.

G F C G Am7
Glo - ry to God, glo - ry to God,
F C G F C
glo - ry to God for - ev - er. We sing: Glo - ry to God,
G Am7 F C G
glo - ry to God, glo - ry to God for - ev - er.
F C G Am7 F C
Glo - ry to God, glo - ry to God, glo - ry to God for - ev - er.

G F C G Am
Take my life and let it be all for You and for Your glo - ry.
F C G F C
Take my life and let it be Yours. Take my life and let it be
G Am F C G
all for You and for Your glo - ry. Take my life and let it be Yours. We sing:
Csus C G/C C Csus C G
3fr
Glo - ry to God, glo - ry to God, glo - ry to God for - ev - er.

GOD OF WONDERS

Words and Music by MARC BYRD
and STEVE HINDALONG

Dsus
Em
Csus2
glo - ry to the Lord on high.
I will call Your name by night.
G
D
God of won - ders be - yond our gal - ax - y,
You are
Am7
Csus2
ho - ly,
ho - ly.
The
G
D
u - ni - verse de - clares Your maj - es - ty.
You are

Am7
Csus2
ho - ly,
ho - ly;
Lord of heav - en and earth,
1
Dsus
Em
Lord of heav - en and earth.
Csus2
Dsus
Em
Csus2

2
Am7
Hal - le - lu - jah to the
C
Lord of heav - en and earth.
Am7
Hal - le - lu - jah to the
C
Lord of heav - en and earth.
Am7
Hal - le - lu - jah to the
C
Lord of heav - en and earth.
G

THE HEART OF WORSHIP

Words and Music by
MATT REDMAN

Em7 D/F♯ A7sus
I'll bring You more than a song, for a song in it - self
Em7 D/F♯ A7sus Em7 D/F♯
is not what You have re - quired. You search much deep - er with - in
A7sus Em7 D/F♯
through the way things ap - pear; You're look - ing in - to my heart.
A7sus D(add2) A/C♯
I'm com - ing back to the heart of wor - ship, and it's

Em9
D/F♯
Gmaj7
A7sus
D(add2)
all a - bout You,_ all a - bout You,_ Je - sus. I'm sor - ry, Lord, for the thing_
A/C♯
Em9
D/F♯
_ I've made_ it, when it's all a - bout You,_
Gmaj7
A7sus
1
Dsus2
D/A
A
all a - bout You,_ Je - sus._
Em7
A7sus
2
D

HERE I AM TO WORSHIP

Words and Music by
TIM HUGHES

E
B/D♯
4fr
Here I am to wor - ship, here I am to bow down, here I am to
E/G♯
Asus2
E
say that You're my God. You're al - to - geth - er love - ly, al - to - geth - er
B/D♯
4fr
E/G♯
To Coda
wor - thy, al - to - geth - er won - der - ful to me.
1
Asus2
B7sus
2fr
2
Asus2
And I'll nev -

B/D♯
E/G♯
A
Asus2
B/D♯
E/G♯
- er know how much it cost to see my sin up - on
1
A
Asus2
2
A
Asus2
D.S. al Coda
that cross. And I'll nev - that cross. Here I am to
CODA
Asus2
B7sus
E

HOLY IS THE LORD

Words and Music by CHRIS TOMLIN
and LOUIE GIGLIO

B♭/D
E♭sus2
Fsus
F
C
6fr
how awe - some is He.
And to - geth - er we sing:
E♭(add2)
B♭/D
E♭sus2
Fsus
Ho - ly is the Lord God Al - might - y; the earth
Gm7
E♭sus2
Fsus
F
B♭/D
E♭sus2
is filled with His glo - ry. Ho - ly is the Lord God Al - might -
Fsus
Gm7
E♭sus2
Fsus
- y; the earth is filled with His glo - ry, the earth

Gm7 E♭sus2 Fsus B♭ E♭sus2
6fr
To Coda
is filled with His glo - ry. We stand and lift up our hands,
Fsus F Gm7 E♭sus2 Fsus F
for the joy of the Lord is our strength.
B♭ E♭sus2 Fsus F Gm7 E♭sus2
We bow down and wor - ship Him now; how great, how awe - some is He.
Fsus F C E♭(add2)
And to - geth - er we sing, ev - 'ry - one

C
E♭(add2)
6fr
D.S. al Coda
CODA
Fsus
sing:
Ho - ly is the
- ry. Yeah, it's ris -
B♭
F/A
A♭(add2)
4fr
- ing up all a - round; it's the an - them of the Lord's
E♭
3fr
B♭
F/A
re - nown. It's ris - ing up all a - round; it's the an -
A♭(add2)
4fr
E♭
3fr
- them of the Lord's re - nown. To - geth - er we sing,

C
E♭
C
E♭
3fr
and ev-'ry - one sing: Ho - ly is the
B♭/D
E♭sus2
Fsus
Gm7
E♭sus2
6fr
Lord God Al - might - y; the earth is filled with His glo -
Fsus
F
B♭/D
E♭sus2
Fsus
- ry. Ho - ly is the Lord God Al - might - y; the earth
Gm7
E♭sus2
Fsus
Gm7
E♭sus2
is filled with His glo - ry, the earth is filled with His glo -

Fsus Gm7 E♭sus2 F
- ry, the earth is filled with His glo - ry.
Gm7(add4) Fsus/A B♭sus2 F Gm7(add4) Fsus/A B♭sus2
F Gm7(add4) Fsus/A B♭sus2 F
Ho - ly, ho - ly is the Lord Al - might - y.
Gm7(add4) Fsus/A B♭sus2 F
Ho - ly, ho - ly.
Repeat and Fade
Optional Ending
B♭

HOSANNA

Words and Music by
BROOKE FRASER

Em
- ry com - ing on the clouds with fire;
- tion ris - ing up to take their place
Am7
the whole earth shakes, the whole earth shakes.
with self - less faith, self - less faith.
D
G
I see His love and mer -
I see a near re - vi -
Em
- cy wash - ing o - ver all our sin;
- val stir - ring as we pray and sing;

Am7
D
the peo - ple sing, the peo - ple sing.
we're on our knees, on our knees.
Ho - san -
cresc.
G/B
C
D
Em7
C
Em7
- na, ho - san - na, ho - san - na in the high - est.
f
D
G/B
C
D
Em7
To Coda
Ho - san - na, ho - san - na, ho -
C
D
1
Em7
san - na in the high - est.

2
Em7
G
Am
Bm
C
D
Heal my heart and make it clean,
G
Em7
o - pen up my eyes to the things un - seen.

C D Em7
Show me how to love like You have loved me.
G/B C D Em7
Ho - san - na, ho - san - na, ho -
mp
C Em7 D G/B C
san - na in the high - est. Ho - san - na, ho - san -
mf
D Em7 C D G
D.S. al Coda
- na, ho - san - na in the high - est. Ho - san -
cresc.

CODA
C
D
Em7
san - na in the high - est,
ho -
C
D
Gsus2
san - na in the high - est.
Em7
Csus2
3fr
G5
3fr

HOSANNA
(Praise Is Rising)

Words and Music by PAUL BALOCHE
and BRENTON BROWN

C
N.C.
we turn to You.
we turn to You.
f
G
Hope is stir - ring,
In Your king - dom
mf
C
hearts are yearn - ing for You,
bro - ken lives are re - newed;
N.C.
we long for You.
You make us new.
'Cause when we see
f

D
Am7
G
You, we find strength to face the day.
D
Am7
In Your pres - ence, all our fears are washed a - way,
Csus2
3fr
C6
Gsus
3fr
washed a - way. Ho - san -
G
C
na, ho - san - na!
You are the God

G
D
Am7
who saves us,
wor - thy of all
our prais - es.
C
Gsus
3fr
G
Ho - san - na,
ho -
C
san - na!
Come, have Your way
Em
D
a - mong us.
We wel - come You here,

1
Am7
C
N.C.
Lord Je - sus.
2
C
E5
D
Ho - san - na!
Am7
C
E5

D
Am
C
Ho - san - na!
Ho -
Gsus
G
Cmaj9
C
san - na,
ho - san - na,
ho -
mp
Gsus/D
G/D
C(add2)/E
san - na,
ho - san -
Lead vocal ad lib.
cresc.
Fsus2
Gsus
G
na. Ho - san - na,
ho -
3fr
f

C
san - na! Come, have Your way
Em
D
a - mong us. We wel - come You here,
Am7
C
E5
Lord Je - sus.
D
Am7
C6
Ho - san - na!

E5
D
Am7
Ho - san -
C6
N.C.
na!

HOW GREAT IS OUR GOD

Words and Music by CHRIS TOMLIN,
JESSE REEVES and ED CASH

* *Recorded a half step lower.*

Bm7
and dark - ness tries to hide. It trem - bles at His voice,
Fa - ther, Spir - it, Son, the Li - on and the Lamb,
Gmaj7
trem - bles at His voice. How great
Li - on and the Lamb.
D
Bm7
is our God! Sing with me: How great is our God!
Gmaj7
A
And all will see how great, how great is our God!

D
1
2
And
Bm7
Name a - bove all names,
wor - thy of all praise.
Gmaj7
A
My heart will sing: How great is our God!
D
2
A
is our God!

D
How great is our God!
Bm7
Sing with me: How great is our God!
Gmaj7
A
And all will see how great, how great is our God!
1, 2 D
3 D
How great

HOW GREAT THOU ART

Words and Music by
STUART K. HINE

*Author's original lyrics are "works" and "mighty."

Additional Verses

3. And when I think that God, His Son not sparing,
Sent Him to die, I scarce can take it in;
That on the cross, my burden gladly bearing,
He bled and died to take away my sin.

4. When Christ shall come with shout of acclamation
And take me home, what joy shall fill my heart!
Then I shall bow in humble adoration
And there proclaim: My God, How great Thou art!

IN CHRIST ALONE

Words and Music by KEITH GETTY
and STUART TOWNEND

G D/F♯ Asus A D/F♯ G Bm7
love, what depths of peace when fears are stilled, when striv - ings
cross as Je - sus died, the wrath of God was sat - is -
stands in vic - to - ry, sin's curse has lost its grip on
(D.S.) hell, no scheme of man, can ev - er pluck me from His
Asus A G D G A D/F♯
cease! My Com - fort - er, my All in All, here in the
fied. For ev - 'ry sin on Him was laid; here in the
me. For I am His and He is mine, bought with the
hand. Till He re - turns or calls me home, here in the
To Coda
1-3
4
D.S. al Coda
(verse 4)
G D/F♯ Em7 G/A D A7sus D G D D/F♯
love of Christ I stand. In Christ a -
death of Christ I live. There in the
pre-cious blood of Christ. No guilt in
pow'r of Christ I'll stand. No pow'r of
CODA
D D/F♯ G D/F♯ Em7 G/A D
stand. Here in the pow'r of Christ I'll stand.
rit.

JESUS MESSIAH

Words and Music by CHRIS TOMLIN,
JESSE REEVES, DANIEL CARSON
and ED CASH

** Recorded a half step lower.*

C/G
F
C/G
Fsus2
Love so a-maz - ing,
love so a-maz - ing.
C
Je-sus Mes-si - ah,
Name a-bove all
mf
F
C
names.
Bless-ed Re-deem - er,
Gsus
Em-man - u-el.
The res-cue for sin-

C
F
ners, the ran - som from heav - en.
C/E
Gsus
C
To Coda
Je - sus Mes - si - ah, Lord of all.
C
Dm7
His bod - y the bread, His blood the wine,
C/E
F
C
bro - ken and poured out, all for love. The whole earth trem - bled and the

Dm7
C/G
F
veil was torn.
Love so a - maz - ing,
C/G
Fsus2
D.S. al Coda
love so a - maz - ing,
yeah.
Je - sus Mes - si -
CODA
Dm7
C/E
All our hope is in You,
all our hope
F
Gsus
Dm7
is in You.
All the glo - ry to You,

C/E
F
Gsus
God,
the Light of the world.
C
F
Je - sus, Mes - si - ah,
Name a - bove all names.
mp
C
Gsus
Bless-ed Re-deem - er,
Em - man - u - el.
cresc.
C
The res - cue for sin - ners,
the ran - som from heav -
mf

F
C/E
Gsus
- en. Jesus Messi - ah, Lord of all.
C
F/A
C/G
Gsus
Jesus Messi - ah, Lord of all.
F
You're the Lord of all,
C
the Lord of all.

LEAD ME TO THE CROSS

Words and Music by
BROOKE FRASER

Gmaj7
D
A/C♯
for my ran - som.
now You're ris - en.
Em
A
Ev - 'ry - thing I once held dear, I count
Bm7
A
Gmaj7
it all as loss. Lead me to the cross
D
A
where Your love poured out. Bring me to my knees,

Gmaj7
D
A
Bm7
Lord, I lay me down.
Rid me of my - self,
Gmaj7
D
A
Em9
I be - long to You.
Oh, lead me,
Gmaj7
A
1
Bm7
A
Gmaj7
D
lead me to the cross.
mf
Bm7
A
G6
D
2
Bm7

Bm
Gmaj7
D
Gmaj7
A
To Your heart, to Your
D
Gmaj7
A
D
Gmaj7
heart, lead me to Your heart,
A
D
Gsus2
A
lead me to Your heart. Lead me to the cross
Gmaj7
D
A
where Your love poured out. Bring me to my knees,

Gmaj7
D
A
Bm7
Lord, I lay me down.
Rid me of myself,
Gmaj7
D
A
I belong to You.
Oh, lead me,
1
Em9
Gmaj7
A
lead me. Lead me to the cross
2
Em9
Gmaj7
A
N.C.
lead me to the cross.

YOU ARE MY KING
(Amazing Love)

Words and Music by
BILLY JAMES FOOTE

D
G
D
A-maz-ing love, how can it be
that You, my King, would die for me?
Asus
A
G/A
3fr
D
G
A-maz-ing love, I know it's true;
D
To Coda
1, 3
Asus
A
G/A
3fr
it's my joy to hon - or You.
2
Asus
A
G
A
D
In all I do, I hon-or You.

You are my King.
You are my King. Jesus, You are my
King. Jesus, You are my King.
D.S. al Coda
(with repeats)
CODA
Asus
A
G
A
D
In all I do, I hon - or You.

MIGHTY TO SAVE

Words and Music by BEN FIELDING
and REUBEN MORGAN

Recorded a half step lower.

G
Em7
Dsus
D
- ness, the kind - ness of a Sav - ior, the hope of na - tions.
Csus2
3fr
Dsus
Csus2/E
D/F#
G
Sav - ior, He can move the
D
Cmaj9
G
Em7
D
moun - tains. My God is might - y to save, He is might - y to save. For -
G
D
Cmaj9
G
To Coda
ev - er Au - thor of sal - va - tion, He rose and con - quered the grave, Je - sus

Em7
D
Cmaj9
G(add2)
con-quered the grave.
Em7
Dsus
Csus2
3fr
So take me as You find
G
Em7
Dsus
D
me, all my fears and fail - ures; fill my life a - gain.
Csus2
3fr
G
Em7
I give my life to fol - low ev-'ry-thing I be-lieve in. Now

D.S. al Coda
Dsus
D
Csus2
3fr
Dsus
Csus2/E
D/F♯
I sur - ren - der,
yes, I sur-ren - der.
CODA
Em7
D
C
G
con - quered the grave.
Shine Your light and let the whole world
D
Em
C
G
D
see we're sing-ing for the glo - ry of the ris - en King. Je - sus,
C
G
D
Em
shine Your light and let the whole world see we're sing - ing

C G D G
for the glo - ry of the ris - en King. Sav - ior, He can move the
D/G Cmaj7 G/B Em D
moun - tains. My God is might - y to save, He is might - y to save. For -
G D Cmaj7 G/B
ev - er Au - thor of sal - va - tion, He rose and con - quered the grave, Je - sus
G/D G
con - quered the grave. You're my Sav - ior, You can move the

D Cmaj9 G Em7 D
moun - tains. God, You are might - y to save, You are might - y to save. For -
G D Cmaj9 G
ev - er Au - thor of sal - va - tion, You rose and con - quered the grave, yes, You
Em7 D Cmaj9
con - quered the grave.
G(add2) Cmaj9 G/D D7 G
You are might - y to save.
rit.

SING TO THE KING

Words and Music by
BILLY JAMES FOOTE

Life and sal - va - tion His em - pire shall bring,
We'll join in sing - ing with all the re - deemed,
and joy to the na - tions when
'cause Sa - tan is van - quished and
Je - sus is King.
Je - sus is King.
1
2, 3
Come, let us sing a song, a

F♯m7
Asus2
song de - clar - ing that we be - long to Je - sus.
E
Oh, and He is all we need,
Dsus2
E
yeah, yeah. Oh, lift up a heart of praise.
F♯m7
Asus2
Sing now with voic - es raised to Je - sus, oh.

To Coda
E
Sing to the King.
E5
D.S. al Coda
CODA
E
King.
Oh, just sing to the King,
sing to the
King.

THE STAND

Words and Music by
JOEL HOUSTON

A
You stood be - fore my fail - ure, and
I walk up - on sal - va - tion, Your
D
car - ried the cross for my shame. My
Spir - it a - live in me. This
A/C♯
F♯m7
sin weighed up - on Your shoul - ders, my soul now
life to de - clare Your prom - ise, my soul now
D
to stand.
to stand.
So what could I say?

E/D
Bm9
F♯m
E/F♯
What could I do,
F♯m
D
E/D
but of - fer this heart, O God,
A/E
E
F♯m
E/F♯
1
F♯m
Bm/F♯
com - plete - ly to You? So
2
F♯m
D
E/D
So what could I say?

Bm9
F#m
E/F#
A
And what could I ___ do, ___
but of - fer this heart, _
Bm7
E
F#m
___ O God, __
com - plete - ly ________ to You? _
D
A
E
F#m7
So I'll stand with arms high and heart a - ban - doned,
mp – mf
D
A
E
F#m7
D
A
in awe of the One who gave it all. I'll stand, my

E F#m7 1 D A E F#m7
soul, Lord, to You sur - ren - dered. All I am is Yours.
2 D A E F#m7 D A
All I am is Yours.
So I'll stand with
cresc.
f
E F#m7 D A E F#m7
arms high and heart a - ban - doned, in awe of the One who gave it all.
D A E F#m7 1 D A
I'll stand, my soul, Lord, to You sur - ren - dered. All I am is Yours.

E F#m7
2
D A
All I am is Yours.
E D A E F#m7
So I'll stand with arms high and heart a - ban - doned,
mp
D A E F#m7 D A
in awe of the One who gave it all. I'll stand, my
rit. poco a poco
E F#m7 D A E
soul, Lord, to You sur - ren - dered. All I am is Yours.

YOUR GRACE IS ENOUGH

Words and Music by
MATT MAHER

Fm7
D♭
You wres - tle with the sin - ner's rest - less heart.
You use the weak to lead the strong.
A♭
A♭/C
You lead us by still wa - ters in -
You lead us in the song of Your
D♭
Fm7
- to mer - cy, and noth - ing can
sal - va - tion, and all Your peo -
E♭
D♭
B♭m7
keep us a - part.
- ple sing a - long.
So re - mem - ber Your

A♭/C
D♭
E♭
Fm7
peo - ple, re - mem - ber Your chil - dren, re - mem - ber Your
E♭
A♭/C
D♭
E♭/D♭
D♭
A♭
prom - ise, O God. Your grace is e - nough,
cresc.
f
E♭
Fm7
D♭
Your grace is e - nough, Your
A♭
E♭
To Coda
1
D♭
grace is e - nough for me.

2
D♭
D.S. al Coda
Yeah, Your
CODA
D♭
B♭m7
A♭/C
3fr
Re - mem - ber Your peo - ple, re -
mf
D♭
E♭
3fr
Fm7
mem - ber Your chil - dren, re - mem - ber Your
E♭/G
3fr
A♭
4fr
D♭
A♭
4fr
prom - ise, O God.
Your grace is e - nough,

E♭ Fm7 D♭ A♭
3fr 4fr
Your grace is e - nough, Your grace is e - nough
E♭ D♭ E♭/D♭ D♭
3fr
for me. Yeah, Your
cresc.
A♭ E♭ Fm7
4fr 3fr
grace is e - nough, Heav - en reach - ing down to us.
I'm cov - ered in Your love.
f
D♭ A♭ E♭
4fr 3fr
Your grace is e - nough for me.

1
2
D♭
God, I see Your
A♭
E♭
For me.
Fm7
D♭
A♭
It's e - nough for me.
E♭
Fm7
A♭/D♭
A♭
4fr
3fr

YOU NEVER LET GO

Words and Music by MATT REDMAN
and BETH REDMAN

* Recorded a half step lower.

F/A
storms of this life, I won't turn back; I know You are near.
til that day comes, we'll live to know You here on the earth.
Am
G
And I will fear no e -
C
Am
G
vil, for my God is with
C
Am
G
me. And if my God is with

C
G
me, whom then shall I fear, whom then shall I
F
C
fear? Oh, no, You nev - er let go,
through the calm and through the storm.
Am7
Oh, no, You nev - er let go, in
ev - 'ry high and ev - 'ry low.
G
To Coda
Oh, no, You nev - er let go,

1
F
C5
3fr
Lord, You nev - er let go of me.
Gsus
3fr
G
F
2
F
And I can see a
Lord, You nev - er let go of me. You
C
Gsus
3fr
G
F
D.S. al Coda
keep on lov - ing and You nev - er let go.
Sing - ing:
CODA
F
C5
3fr
Lord, You nev - er let go of me.

Gsus
3fr
G
F
C
Yes, I can see a light that is com-ing for the
C/E
Am7
heart that holds on. And there will be an end to these trou-bles, but un-
G
til that day comes, still I will praise You,
F
C5
3fr
still I will praise You.

Gsus
Fsus2
C
Oh, no, You nev - er let go,
through the calm and through the storm.
Am7
Oh, no, You nev - er let go, in
ev - 'ry high and ev - 'ry low.
G
Oh, no, You nev - er let go,
F
Lord, You nev - er let go of me.
C
Oh, no, You nev - er let go,

Am7
through the calm and through the storm. Oh, no, You nev - er let go, in
G
ev - 'ry high and ev - 'ry low. Oh, no, You nev - er let go,
F
C5
Csus
C
Lord, You nev - er let go of me.
Gsus
F
C
Lord, You nev - er let go of me.